DARK-ROOM

THE BRITTINGHAM PRIZE IN POETRY

DARK-ROOM

JAZZY DANZIGER

THE UNIVERSITY OF WISCONSIN PRESS

The University of Wisconsin Press
1930 Monroe Street, 3rd Floor
Madison, Wisconsin 53711-2059
uwpress.wisc.edu

3 Henrietta Street
London WCE 8LU, England
eurospanbookstore.com

Printed in the United States of America

Library of Congress Cataloging-in-Publication Data
Danziger, Jazzy.
  Darkroom / Jazzy Danziger.
      p.   cm. — (The Brittingham prize in poetry)
  Poems.
  ISBN 978-0-299-28684-2 (pbk. : alk. paper)
  ISBN 978-0-299-28683-5 (e-book)
  I. Title. II. Series: Brittingham prize in poetry (Series).
  PS3604.A593D37   2012
  811'.6—dc23
                              2011041963

for Sharon Kay Garrett Danziger

Contents

Acknowledgments

Grateful acknowledgment is made to the following journals and anthologies where these poems first appeared:

Bellingham Review: "Darkroom"

Beloit Poetry Journal: "Yahrzeit"

Boxcar Poetry Review: "*The Sacrifice of Isaac* (Uffizi)"

Mid-American Review: "Earthquake in Wabash Valley, Three Months Before Our Engagement"

The Minnesota Review: "Cafeteria," "The Discarded"

Southern Indiana Review: "First Touch"

Two Weeks: "Orlando"

Washington Square: "Found"

The Written Wardrobe: "The Psychiatrist's Teen Daughter Self-Evaluates"

For their invaluable assistance with *Darkroom*, I would like to thank Rita Dove and Gregory Orr, as well as Andrew Gallagher, Kathryn Exoo, Kerri Webster, and Mary Jo Bang.

I remain especially grateful to those who offered close readings of many of these poems: Christa Romanosky, Yasmine Dalena, Steve Barbaro, Carolyn Creedon, Paul Legault, Mark Parlette, Jasmine V. Bailey, Mark Wagenaar, Sam Taylor, Lisa Fink, Jonterri Gadson, Cecilia Llompart, Wanling Su, Zayne Turner, Megan Fishmann, Alex Penn, Joe Thomas, Sebastian Deken, Andrew Hobin, and Emily Flanders. Thanks also go to the University of Wisconsin Press, Ron Wallace, and Jean Valentine, as well as Dad, Max, Nandy, and Lynda. And to my students at the University of Virginia for their bold and beautiful work, which played a crucial role in my own poetic education.

Lastly, to Brian Loyal—first reader, always.

I

Florida Poems

Orlando

On Monday, a man chased his son through the street,
and with a sword carved his body out
while the neighbors watched.

I was washing my face. The faucet flooded the sink
with white salt and tidesoap. As always, the soil
was purl-stitched, loosely tangled

in coast-cloth. Oranges grew only to rot
and scour the whites from our teeth.
That boy was not the first to be sunk

in Florida soil. Days before, a young woman
duct taped a baby's mouth, placed heart-shaped stickers
in her hair, and dropped her in a bassinet

of dirt and brushwood. The meter reader who found her
can no longer eat or work. This, here,
every day. Another child.

A lexis of murder, flatness,
fire. And the words like a friction, numbing
all human hide. I think we won't know

what we've lost. Like our southernness. So pale,
the Georgians upstairs don't have the heart to object
when we claim it. Or our sense

of distance. No mountains rise here
and by their blue color show you
how far and how small you are—

here you notice only what the strip mall road
can offer up—fox paws for science class shelves.
The wonder that the mammalian wild remain

where there is nothing wild to roam.
Listen: I can't see the Atlantic from Orlando.
But I'm close enough to hear it calling—

a rush through the valves, a slosh when I dig deep enough,
planting a prize petunia. It's leaking. Everywhere.
Promising to whittle me down to my spine.

Guilt

Playing Nintendo with a boy the next
neighborhood over, you accidentally
stayed out past dark. Remember being lost,
your mother's voice

a cricket's, helpless to direct you.
This was her punishment for being beautiful, for sleeping
in her madness; let that moment when you ran home at dusk
belong to seven as it belongs to her thirty-seven,

let the New Year shut closed the open wound,
like the one unfastened by a barefoot sprint home,
after dark, when you hadn't told her you'd be gone.
But belong to every year. Your absence was not the cause

of her final sorrows, though she howled for you,
though you feel that year cradling you
until there is no mother
but that year. You are opening, in this.

Opening in other memories. With a silver pick,
you once tore Florida grass and mud
from a horseshoe bottom, marveling at the animal's obedience,
the giant ankle bone at perfect rest

in your yellowed palm, his brown-eyed trust, even as you told him
your mother's ankles were weak. That once,
in a northern hotel room, you touched
them lightly; she wept so loudly that you could see

the silver crowns in the back of her teeth.
That was the year of horses' feet, of feeding carrots over fences
to horses now dead,
the velvet round riding hat and its lining

lined like her bones' fractured form, now lined
beneath other horses' feet: northern horses, since our family buried her
where she was born. When they sold the horse
named Sugar, they gave me Lightning. I was thrown

from the saddle: saw fields stretching for miles under eventide,
the black nimbus, the long dark legs rising above the grass,
the wind flattening it, the country sea perpendicular
to the sky. As we prepared to drive home, turning circles

in the parking lot dirt
with "In the Flesh" soft on cassette,
I told her I would never ride again.
That abandonment belongs to ten and forty.

It could not have continued to hurt her in the year
when she threw off the world; I insist, knowing better,
that it could not have been present
when she threw off all that broke her.

Young Family, 1985

In the earliest memory, light
is the circle on your thigh.

The cavern that will form between us three
is not yet a crack. The bedsheet, dry,

crushed and unclean, is stained
by tomato's salt. He worships your taking in

of the vegetable: whole, no use for a knife
or small bites—your mouth barrel-wide,

the ceiling fan reflected in your dentist caps
and crowns. *See, baby? Brush. Silver fills in the spaces*

when we don't sweep badness clean.
Your front teeth push through tightened skin.

He lifts an arm to pull us near,
And we witness the transformation from man

to book. He says this member of *Solanum* lives on
not by its own syrup, but by its willingness to bring forth

the sweetness of richer cuisine. The fruit you enjoy,
philanthropic, noble, round, is in turn aided

by the salt that drowns upon that pointed, wet chin.
In the next room, a bird beats her oiled wing on the windowsill.

You kiss your husband again. Wrapped in the dry sheet,
I lift a pink arm to your face. One of the voices in the room says,

So happy, and think: All of these years before us,
a line of stones not yet weathered or washed,

but uncrushed and clean.

Latitude, with My Mother

Ringing the footplate breeds a small ocean, the top of the cochlea
      running like a bath. I heard the sound of the fruit tree
      dropping orange beads

without want. Heard the oak, whose roots dipped below our pool.
      Each time the porch chimes moved,
      the tree moved. The kitchen tiles moved,

the foundation moved—all were dipping,
      coiling into a bowl, slowly, so as not to scare.
      But I was scared. These nights, I wanted

her wet hair on my cheek. It was *Baby, I can't*
      turn over to hold you. She was comfortable
      waiting, falling asleep to the sound

of dripping trees, forgetting to listen for my father
      to come home, shuffling the mail between his hands in the dark.
      When a dog barks, I believe he knows something

that I can't know. The process is chemical.
      Some old survival system is a ruined temple
      in my blood. Do you see the statue of a woman

with her ear against the stony wall,
      believing the long, distant rumble of a ship
      is the planet knocked from its course?

When it's quiet, I call it "calm," and wait
      for the crack of the wooden joint, the wash
      of a once-small ocean, now the darling baby

of a continent's ear, the low, defiant vibration
      of ground come to conquer.

Horseshoe

Mrs. Rivera and her son were fighting in the kitchen.
"*Idiota*," she said, spooning out clams
and yellow rice. "Like *la rubia*, that friend
of your sister's." That was the end
of her pet name for me. She forgot
that I lay barefoot, belly-down, one room over,
barely seven. Oh, sorry, oh, sorry she said

when she heard me cough, but the family
continued the teasing all winter. They'd remind me
of my sick mother, of the neighborhood kids
discovering I didn't know "Silent Night," or the meaning
of the lamb. I'd asked why plastic sheep
were grazing on the lawns all December.

One morning, the Riveras made jewelry for their children.
They covered the good dining table with wires,
beads and wax charms. We stood in clusters
at each corner; the father's black curls bounced
with each clip of the pliers. He looked at me,
held up two necklaces:
            one held a horseshoe charm, blue
and waxy, the other, the addition symbol,
uneven, long—
            the cross. I knew nothing
but its shape, bisecting lines that pleased them,

this family that could rise from bed, meet for meals,
crinkle tissue-thin Bible paper with their fingers. This family:
sometimes, their house was all I had.
Their father asked me which necklace
I preferred. I pointed to the one
the other children wore.

        They laughed,

all of them, licking their mouths,
the mother howling, "*Rubia*, take the horseshoe,
your mother will prefer it."

Months later, Mrs. Arlen down the street
was offended by the Rivera children.
She swooped in, her red hair piled high

like leaves, her massive body sweating,
her face shiny and wet, the mouth opening
to tell Juanita that if she rammed her bike
against their dumpster again,
she'd tell her mother on her so fast
it would make all of our heads spin.
To be abused so by an adult—the fear
could manifest only in laughter,
a great mock joy hiding the new knowledge
of our smallness.

We echoed the phrase
for weeks: me, twisting my head so far around,
owl-like, that sometimes I thought
it would leave blood-red bruises
on my collarbone.

Miscarriage

Who is this straggler?

       Maggie's body surrenders one last pup
near the chair. Jewel-tight, it's sacked, balmed
by departure. So Mom is reminded of loss;

so we are reminded in each sigh, each long look
at Maggie, our senses churning until they turn

like clotted cream. The days swell sickly. Heat floats
on morning milk, unpasteurized, fat, and Mom dusts
the old miscarriage cards—
                        that aging and ductless sympathy,
older than us, the many bloodshot birds on vellum.

She is my Mama, broad-backed machine of grief, greased roots,
waking in delirium in dusk, panicked we'll be late for school.
She hid us from the second scene, but we saw
the flour-white pouch, thin border preventing breath,

tissue between life and all else. So often she crawls
into her portrait of that sheet,
so often we look at her and the refusal to rise,
that cold back, wet hair, body becoming
the bed, hear her confessions of old habits:
how she rocks herself backward,

then forward, like tide, her ritual for inviting sleep, because her infant-self
was never touched. Nothing came to move her, she loved only
her own muscle and bone; all was interior, and then the interior failed.

Yahrzeit

I learn the word *leilot*: nights, plural,
a false feminine. How often I've sung *nights*

without knowing what I sing. Each night
you carry me, frozen child, from temple

to the house's citrus heat. You bathe me
in the lowest tub. The body is washed,

dried, dressed. The body is wrapped
in sheets. The light withdraws. The door

slides shut. Your footsteps darken
in the hallway. The child mourns every night,

until mourning is its mother.

The Day After

The morning after you beat me,
before school, it is dark, it is spring, and lonely
on the carpet of Dad's apartment.

The television glows
like the grapefruit I eat each day
at lunch hour. It feels like the same one each day,

brought back from death. In the mornings,
someone in California programs music videos
for the friendless insomniac, or children

on their way to school. Helping us
find treasure in a fresh chord. "Barely Breathing" begins.
It's a song about love, but that title

and I'm thinking about blocks against my throat,
fingernails in my arm. Each part burns.
The song sticks in my head,

plays all day long. I rub my Band-Aid
through my cheap sweater
while we write x and y in pre-algebra, first period.

I have been good. Good at hiding
what I'm afraid of. Afraid
of needing this scar.

The Psychiatrist's Teen Daughter Self-Evaluates

There are two kinds of people
in the world: those who wear pants,

and those who tolerate them. My aversion
to pants was, at first, rooted in an unhealthy

gender bias (as a six-year-old
I found them "unwomanly," horrified

by the women who came into my grandmother's salon
in anything but a skirt) but puberty transformed

the cause of my distaste: a good pair of pants
is unforgiving on a girl with hips. I learned this

at Abercrombie and Fitch—there are two kinds
of customers in that world: those who eat, and those

who are assisted by salesgirls. A lot of my anxiety revolves
around appearance, and it seems that I'm unhappy

with either person I know how to become: the one
who's looked at, and the one who's invisible.

When I was thirteen, Isabella Lombardi taught me
how to get a boy to approach you in the mall:

make eye contact as he comes at you, lock your gaze
on him, then find a bench and sit down.

There are two kinds of boys, she said, those who follow me
and those who follow me. In other words,

she never failed. I failed without her, though,
and one rainy night when we were riding in the back

of Isabella's dad's Jeep my father called and said
there were two types of girls I could choose to become:

the girl who calls her father or the girl
who ends up in a ditch. He didn't mean it

to come out so bad, but I hadn't phoned
in two days. I remember the school production

of *Little Shop of Horrors*. There were two kinds of students
that night: those who sang and danced, and those

who set off the fire alarm. Isabella was the latter,
and she wasn't allowed back to classes.

Three months before my mother died
she bought me a silver dress that was too small for me.

She didn't know this before she said,
"You'll look like Miss America," since there are two ways

to measure a daughter's size: through the forgiving lens of love
and through the pucker of an unforgiving fabric.

She couldn't get the zipper up, so I said,
"You try it on," and she wouldn't,

because she knew it would fit. One afternoon,
she was looking at gold necklaces in Mayor's Jewelers in the mall

while I sat at a wrought-iron table outside of the door,
sipping a milkshake. Four boys came up, as if I was Isabella—

I hadn't even looked at them. They called me "Mama,"
they asked for my phone number. I was scared,

but my mother turned around, saw us,
and shooed them away. I was both of the two girls

I could be in that moment: the frightened
and meek young girl, and the child

who wants her mother to know
someone else has found her baby beautiful.

Mother Invention

In my dream
last night, the man
shooting from a window
on DeMun
was called *ailant*
by a woman
dodging his bullets
from the ground.
I had just crashed
into someone's boxy white car,
and my brother's hands
were bleeding. The gathering crowd,
called forth by an ambulance
bathed in Christmas lights,
was right
for this man's grief.

The word that woman
meant to say
was *assailant*. I didn't know this
in the dream,
that woman
being my creation.

The Visitor

Her camp counselor slides open the door
to the lounge. To prepare this room for her,
he's turned off the lights, drawn the thin curtains,

left a fruit plate on the coffee table, and water, a blanket
on the couch's arm. Artificial, mid-day dark. Now she knows
someone has died. Anything less

would merit a phone call, a warning—
this is a thing said in person, quickly,
a bandage wrenched from the skin.

                                       Something more
there: strange figure, *Dad*—the long flight
from Florida, and he is here mid-summer,

mid-session, made weird by the light
and her surprise. He is crying a little.
She thinks of her brother fallen from a high place.

Thinks of glass-cut skin, of a beating—there is so little time
for imaginings, because she is shaking her father—
she is small and panicked, little animal,

and when he says *Mommy died* it is not the idea that hurts
so much as the words' imprecision, their silliness, the way they fall loosely
around her. Passive

phrase, as if this was out of her mother's control—
she already knows in her body that's false. And the childishness
of *Mommy* when she is fourteen, with her wild crushes on boys.

Yes, it is correct, that word, that babyish thing,
because what she wonders in the first instant
is *Will the boys pay attention to me now?*

Which one will let her cry into his surfer haircut?
Loss, the line dividing *before* from whatever will begin
when she leaves this room. A cup of ice rattles,

the pieces melting in a small bar of sun
through the window. Already, the memory
of that soft voice drops away,
with abandon.

Other Mothers

Something in the echo across the elementary school yard,
the way anemic Florida ice trembles
and falls from science building gutters

and smashes without fanfare.
Worse than being alone
is what being alone means:

no one else's mother
forgot today was a school holiday. No other mother
dropped her daughter off and drove away.
The child thinks of other houses, of baked bread

in clean kitchens with calendars, with today circled
in popsicle-red Sharpie. She thinks of her mother,
back from grocery shopping, falling in the garage,

spilling oranges and bright bottles of liquor
on the concrete floor, her pleated skirt
spread out and soaking.

The dazzling fury of that body, the way
it can blame you for its own mistakes.
The girl will be in trouble

whatever she does. Her voice
would crack this chill, the electric cold—
even the smallest squeak or hum

and she can feel the wooden spoon
on her behind, the back of her head,
whichever bodily arch offers itself up

as she cowers, flat, on the linoleum.
She stands in the parking lot. She wonders what she can do
to save herself. What is the proper way

to be saved? Clutching the braided hat on her head,
fifteen minutes of writhing before she begins
to howl. *Help*, she screams,

someone, please, I don't know what to do
and soon is heard through the glass of a donut shop
well down the street. The owner

scuttles out to her,
shouting *what's wrong what's wrong*
and she is red and wet

from her crying. He takes her hand
across the street, lets her call her mother
from the phone in back, which hangs so high

he must dial for her.
No one answers. He gives her a French cruller,
round, ringlike, on wax paper—

he has cinnamon on his hands. All the patrons are made
of coffee and smoke and Aqua Net. For now, she is allowed to nap,
to disintegrate onto a hard orange booth seat
like fine sugar onto a pastry mat.

II

The Body Erased (Fever Dreams)

On the last whorl they are coarsest on the base, but nowhere sharp or clean cut; the whole surface is covered with a dark olive periostracum, under which the shell is white; aperture ovate, the body erased white, the pillar gyrate but not pervious, the outer lip thin, sharp; the canal rather wide and strongly recurved. The nucleus is not preserved on any of the specimens.

William Healey Dall, "New Species of the Genus Mohnia from the North Pacific," 1913

Darkroom

The body erased. Light birthing the image.

The hand's obstruction removes an eye, a rib.
It happened this way:
                    the soft infrareds not red
but black, engraved in the colloid. The choked look
of the projector, the jam-capped reds of filters
and their choice of *contrast intensity*—darker

and darker, the sooted blood. Color deciding
how white is your white on gloss or matte.
This power trip and scare. We were looking

inside the grain, wrenching the focus knob,
the negative sharpened
but observed through mirrors.

This could have been creation:

the tendon and mouth, blank
of the background bound in the space, were seen;
halide silver and dirt clinging,
separating, finding the natural shape.

Then, we had our desires. And tricks
of the hand and light. We made our demands.
So the salts formed the backs of spoons
or fish scales,

or human smoke. And images in silver
that were not silver: a few teeth flashing
in the soil.

We mangled our subjects after the shot—technique hushing the grain.
    The body had its hunger
and its words, the *agitation*s and *stop bath*s, the vinegar and burn
and fingernails blacked. Our brutal selves reeling
the strips onto spools. The world made new,

and blooming, and dumb.

First Touch

Girls who rise from poolwater dark
rise clean, in white. Flat, medicinal slope
of chests, the low thoracic cage

a fuselage, half-burned. Girls rise. Boys watch
in boxers, thin legs dangling, while cabin lights
boil orange on the camp-top. For now, the *watching*

is the animal, the heart-howling is enough. Lightning
on the horizon, so girls dry themselves, walk
through wet clay to their beds to dream of boys.

One girl dreams in a fever, dreams she is grown,
standing in a Milwaukee rest stop. The man with the gun
is handsome, red-headed, leaning against the bathroom door.

He is polite in asking *do you want this?* She knows to nod
in clammed-up yielding. She cannot curb this womanly body,
this dream. A glass map of Cathedral Square catches the fall,

peels her skin freshly, like husk. The bleed builds
to agreeable warmth. The man says *my baby*, pulls towels
from an aluminum box, wets them, washes her,

puts her together with birdlime,
that glue. No one has touched her like this,
so she forgives the wound. And she is his—

he leaves, and she will wait. It is no longer enough
to be seen. She will always wait
to be opened.

Maps

The bride sings:

In Khartoum, our mouths are full of ice milk.
Love and God and your mother are lifting my shawl
in the ballroom off Nile Road, where ceiling lights
hang like wet cotton.

                     I work at the Coca-Cola plant.
They hire deaf girls to inspect the bottles. It doesn't require
every sense, merely to look on the assembly line
for slight curves in the neck, broken bits of glass
                                 in the body. So there's cola
at our wedding table, and hot butter,
dishes of mutton, white cheese, and bread. And sugar
from Kenana downstream, where canecutters slice
the blistered stalks.

                     Now on the jirtig bed, half-hidden
from guests, we wait for ritual, surround ourselves
with older women. They baked my red heart
each night this month, set me above a wood pit
to roast me thick like meat. My sisters prepared me,
brushed me sore with turmeric, coffee.
They stripped me of hair with lemon juice
and boiled sugar, lit me like a lantern.

I lost my hearing at ten in a schoolhouse.
The explosions down the street shot waves of stars
and dirt and chickens for miles. The heat melted
our plastic book jackets: my skirt stained
bright as a bluebird feather.

In my dream last night, we were wedded in the south.
A man slaughtered a bull for us. Its long tail whipped
in the grass. Its stomach and sides were dark with dirt, and the skin slipped
from its bones. I saw a village boy who had taken a razor
to his hair. He patted himself with ash and clay,
held a cupped hand above his own head filled with water
and cattle urine for bleaching. The liquid spilled down his shoulders,
but the ash and clay slowed it, dried it on his chest. You could map
whatever movement it had made in its short life,
could chart where the rivers had run
through the sheet of earth on his skin.
When I woke, I saw my scars as borders.

Cafeteria

"We want peace—there is something that we are occupied with: growing wheat."

Soviet President Yuri Andropov, April 19, 1983, in response to a letter from ten-year-old American Samantha Smith. Smith's correspondence with Andropov resulted in international celebrity. On the way home from filming a television show in August 1985, Samantha and her father were killed when the plane on which they were flying crashed, killing everyone aboard.

The kindergarteners are hysterical
on the recess field. It seems to them
the right thing to be. They mimic
the way their parents dance
when grieving: all arms
and bobbing heads, a cattle kind of song.
We've been drinking frosted bottles of pop
on the high school side, spreading jam
on bread. The bees keep gathering
in our bottle caps, flying in
from the still-green trees. I've been parading
my work around, peacocking for Beau.
He says, *Don't show me*
that contact sheet. I can't stand
when my friends make art.
So brazen! *Don't question this,* he says
when we hear the news. I'm shaking,
taking a seat on the cold bench
across from him. *Just accept.*
Such bad advice, but he's older, larger,
has been kicked out of school twice
for filling the Erlenmeyer flasks
after hours with milk. I love
his fingers, the asterisks of lines
on the backs of his hands, his fat palms
where his life lines break briefly
before continuing, signaling some future,
recoverable blow.

No word can bring Samantha back.
"Congratulations on your new job,"
she wrote to Andropov. "I have been worrying
about Russia and the United States
getting into a nuclear war."
I don't care what Beau says; I show him

24

what I've made with math. I show him
how I shot my bedroom in 25 steps,
so that the contact sheet made a mosaic
of the room, with black-bordered grids
reading Kodak Tri-X. It's good film,
good grain. Even the mistakes
are good. Look how I've made my world
into measurable space. I have no talent yet
for subtlety. "It seems to me—"
wrote Andropov. "I can tell by your letter—
that you are a courageous and honest girl,
resembling Becky, the friend of Tom Sawyer
in the famous book of your compatriot Mark Twain."
Beau says all artists should be silenced:
art's long need for protagonists
births each human's vanity. I'm embarrassed
for myself. I close my eyes. I see the way
Samantha twirled before the cameras,
how she burned herself into film.
See the white wings descending
below glide slope. The captain's hat
turning east.

Courting

You and your icy lock
beaten back,
your slick deadpan,
your unmoored gaze.
You need a woman
to ask you
a question,
cleft the spangled geode
from your hard,
black heart.
Easy for me to ask
if you get along
with your brother.
He wears
a white rochet, you say,
when carrying full pails,
cold blueberries
in the church yard.
I ask you
is he not afraid
of earthly stains?
Now you look
like you're mine.
I feel
our combined fever
in the track light,
the rumble
from the line.
Javelin-light,
now you always
look back
if I can't keep up
with our group, walking
in map-blind dark.
Sometimes it is better not to know
what obligations we're traveling toward.

The Discarded

A shutter held open long enough
can capture most things. Widened
toward light, waiting for enough
of it, waiting to close. A girl and a boy
in a Jeep
enter a cornfield in the dark.
She makes a loop
in his flannel shirt, instinctive
clutch, the kind newborns know.
What can she expect, seen
through his small aperture, his iris
a rough f-stop? Their courtship,
in this way, is willed to be longest,
thickest of exposures. In the low light,
if her bare arms were lit, you'd see
their lines on the print, slow wrap
around his back. And the wheel,
hard-stopped, growing sugar-black
in its constant position.
Likewise, his disinterested place
in the bucket seat. Sometimes he tells her
she is pretty, with his hands
in her hair, how he'd like to spend a few years
making sandwiches for her in a kitchen,
the quaint linoleum kind. How he'll lovingly
wash and shake-dry her lettuce, slice the bread
into cat's ears every day. A baby crow
out the window, Daddy Crow waiting
for mellowscotch pie. Boiler of syrup,
butter, yolk, his hand over her hand
on the hot aluminum handle. Really,

he does not want these things. Doesn't
even want anyone to know he's here
with her. Just wants that open part.
For her, it is the world.
For him, it is the car. In the field.
After curfew. Families down the road
drawing the farmhouse blinds.

And her weak heart rehearsing,
silently, the half-truth she'll offer
when he's been dodged from her print,
light-blocked from that world.
Well we did nothing
but talk. I kept myself ajar,
but I couldn't capture a thing.

The Island

Because identity could not hold,
men scuttled to shore, ripping egg-weeds
from the ground, pulling crabs from stocking-holes,

shirring the sand in a shallow dish, molding sea-clay
to form pockets of air, playing, beating, destroying
the beachside, wounding the animals who arrived to witness

the boat swelling onto the shore, breaking
into cow-bark or else a substance that has no name,
that dwells and shelters itself in the back room

of the brain. In the brush, a girl appeared in the sunny dress
her mother had bought for the Christmas card. *Please stop scuttling,*
she said. *You'll make the shells ache.*

The men worked on, silent, dragged a sea-log
from the water, waterlogged, dark and sick with wetness.
Their tasks made no sense, just a sense

of displacement, of knowing we had been here before.
On the beach the light twisted until it was no longer night,
until it was the illusion of night.

Then the shallow dish held more than the shell of self,
but less than the beach.

The Shallow Dish Held More

than the shell of self, but less than the beach.
In a spell that school day, I learned
that Winslow Homer painted for his lost souls

the illusion of rescue—a distant boat, black smear
at the ocean's back wall. For each dark man lost at sea,
bound with a bone charm at his neck, the sight like injury

turned white, there reigns the hope of triple-sails behind
a mountain of wave. A God-like thing, canceling out a hull's mess
of shark blood, the ball gown of a waterspout on the horizon.

The teacher thumbed the slide tray, turned us to the ship,
said, *This was for hope.* I wish I could circle back after these years,
stand in my saddle shoes, echo the oil:

that ship will not come. We're called to embrace foreground:
Starvation. A broken keel. The lazy eye of the beast
who curves and flaps his fin, smacks his jaw,

who lifts his hungry heft to the belly of the boat.
I bellow and bray in a teacup,
afloat, unworthy of a painter's vision;

not yet the chaos worthy of control, but something
like the small fisherman behind the orange line of driftwood:
his protection from the ocean-by-oil—

the line which keeps us from retrieving
and, weather-broken, being retrieved.

The Sacrifice of Isaac (Uffizi)

Don't believe the result of Caravaggio's
greatest failure: that one black eye of Isaac
turning to the light—

there's more terror in Abraham's wrinkled hand,
in the curve of ram's-neck above the son's head.
His eye has little fear, no reflection of father pushing knife to neck,

no petrified uncertainty,
but mild offense—imprecise, choked.
Blame—

and blame retracted. We all are guilty of knowing:
the boy survives. Foreknowledge makes us weak.
Comfort warps our illustration, darkens the perception of dread.

Do I do the boy double harm? The more I look, the more my hand
is filled by knife. Yet, see its transparency? The portion of arm
showing through silver blade? Little care. It is nearly as offensive

as the eye. And double Isaac: Boneri—one model for both angel and boy,
double-self hidden by curl and shadow. Never any risk, always the power
to retrieve the weapon, to point one spot-lighted finger toward the animal.

In the painting, the ram draws so near the knife, its fold of sloping ear a cave.
Its pointed snout whispers to Isaac: *I give myself for you. I must
give myself for you.*

The true ram was captured in a thicket below the rare landscape,
locked to ground by human strength, throat slit, an animal scream rising,
a curdled wail, then the flow of blood for worship, blood for blood's sake,

dark, bubbling hot. There is truth in that framing,
but little easy beauty.

The Re-Telling

All children recraft it, restitch the sad work
of their mothers. In time, I knead your suicide
into myth, embroider the low embarrassment,
framing you in wet-thorned lilies, with scarlet stitch.

In this wish, it still happens: you drop
at the white glow of gun. As you slump,
blonde, whiskey-bleached, a sack of person,
a northern horse rides through, runs his reddened snout

across your wet mane. His coat leaves you
coppered. The staff of the nursing home—in whose parking lot
you fall—arrives through the orange trees. White heels clicking,
they are shuffling off to buy milk

and medicines in brown paper bags. The doctor
has been disorderly, and the pantry is bare.
Orange oils drip onto their starched white nursing uniforms.
They are accustomed to death there:

the elderly depart daily. You chose this place, as if to say
This was natural. As if your place of departure
could define the cause. One of their hands
traces yours, then connects

to your back, props you up on maple's bark.
Your wedding hand lifts from the lake.
Florida twilight makes all purple,
and the cross they place beside you, not knowing who

or what you are, whether you believe in their God
or mine, is placed. As if you never cut a piece of red paper
as a stand-in for the ram's blood.
Tonight I believe this myth: that I,

who had traveled to camp that summer,
cracked open the bedroom door of a hundred-year-old building
and told the damp hallway *I know there's a reason
I can't sleep.* I waited for the response
in a cloud of clay and dust.

My feet collected soot from the tile, my night-hours made me
more wolf than girl, so I wrapped a section of nightgown
in my hand, and chewed the end, doglike, until I could sleep.
The next day, they told me the news.

Your voice tonight, boiling, odd, thick like milk,
rings like a bell, each peal superior to the last.
Tonight, your myth reforms once again.
Tonight, at the urging of my love,

your blood becomes the ram's blood of the holiday plate:
a paper left too long in the sun.

Muscle color seeping out
in strange vapor.

Found

We cleaned out your apartment.
I took nothing. Nothing fit.
We gave your shoes
to the secretaries. Piled
trash bags of makeup,
loofahs, faux petits fours
from a tray held
by a ceramic dog. I was
suspicious, even of
the cooking sherry. I looked
for clues. I was the first
to find your Hebrew day-planner,
and the 8th day of Av, 5759:
Get over my fear of guns.

After Looking at the Blackboard
2005

After looking at the blackboard
the professor says something in Japanese.
My smile at his joke about *horizonti* is turned
like an unbaked pie. Abruptly,
the snow of the chalk that says
ROOT TEST,
end-color of the bleach Daddy and I bought you
each Thursday for your laundry
(though you asked for so much that,
yes,
we joked you drank it—
isn't that funny?)
the powdered words appear in a line of vision
that belies twenty years, and there it is:
the smile whipped into paste at the epiphany
that in these six years, I have never before
felt so clearly
your absence.

Dream: Vienna, Illinois

My mother returned to me
after months of muted sleep. We rode in her blue Chevy.
She earned it, selling soup to the people of Vienna,

a city pronounced inelegantly, distinguishing itself
from its foreign twin. I would not recognize her face:
she was all eyes, elbows, a shape floating near those distinct seatbelt buckles

with the letters "GM" in black. I resented her telling me
what they stood for, preferring my imagination. This was all
imagination. I knew her by the juvenile popping of her gum, was thrown

by the maternal Afghan in her lap, her drunken hand on the leather gearshift.
We passed the small wooded area at the corner of the stoplights on Maitland
and Sandspur. She said, "Let me tell you what I saw today:

two bodies in wet cement, a man and a woman,
lying there in a gray puddle, shoved through the machine
by someone they knew. The woman had no arms, no legs. I hated her

for ruining that beauty."
Her face turned wine, matched her mouth; I didn't know
what angered her. She pulled near the junkyard where they slept:

cars slowed, flashlights passed over the bodies, lights like ships
lost in a harbor; the violence of the moment subdued
by a lack of the color you would expect when

two lovers are torn from the body.
I wanted to write it. I tried to keep my ears open—
could try only so long before it was all sea shells or

mountains destroying any shred of the new that I seek
here each week. I tried to rhyme: tried to understand how the chip in her teeth

could hint at my grief. Through the cracked veneer she whistled,

you'll never get it to the page.
Before I could wake, she drove me to her tiny house
near the railroad track. I was welcomed with a turn

of the dark knobs on the television set, a gift
of gold hoops, a sip of the soup she couldn't sell.

As she poured it, thick, into a bowl too detailed
to be some remnant of my day,
she stirred with a broken pencil.

III

Natural Disasters

Earthquake in Wabash Valley,
Three Months Before Our Engagement

The birds don't freeze mid-air. Still, I'm shaken
from bed. Half-awake I stand, call for you
and the chattering of cheap silver in our drawer.
I thought I had heard all the sounds

the world could offer. The morning is so dark,
the noise could skin me clean.

                              The four walls groan,
pull away, make new maps of my position in the doorframe.
Streetlamps rattle in Missouri-wet lanes. Fault-myths

come to nothing:

black coal barges ride southward on the river,
bells in northern churches don't peal. But plates are moving,

caressing plates, like my science teacher said in school: Take
your mother's bridal china to the lake, let one saucer slide

over another. Go, make material an incalculable love.
The oldest mountains are evidence of many

forgotten battles, of limestone cleaved. Shock
of new color in the history of a soil. A karst topography
upon which I picture you,

nearly feel you and your boyish dread, a wedding hand
feverish and reaching,

but I'm alone again in the aftershock. Even the land
can't marry the houses.

The First Wound (1996 and 1964)

One night we drove the circle
in search of our escaped hounds.
Her breath made panicked circles on the hot window.
She lied: What will your father think?
With all this rain, their fur will smell and stick
on the leather cream seats.
The lie was like a sugar cube.

On the third loop, she said
she had once been taken into the woods.

School friends had left her shivering near the bus stop,
a cold lunch pail in her mittened paw.
It was the old lost puppy trick, and she would never cease
to be a sucker for a misplaced animal.

She said she was "torn apart," but could not explain
what prompted such a confession. She said
the glue of her body softened, and she stumbled home,
a tangle of soot-covered sticks and wet ground, and,
of course,
no one believed her.

From then on, no dark place
was a place toward which I wandered.

I remember, later that year:
My helmet stained with oil soap,
my affinity for the shoe pick. I cleaned hooves
longer than I rode. I left little time for riding.

It was the English style—the clomp of hooves that way—
it sounded like a packed train. No room for anyone new,
and I would be lucky to get a leg over.
Sensing my need to ride like no one had ridden before,
she said, in her way, *it is our destiny*
to repeat the life that came before ours.

You are not your own.

Dream: Young Family II

She fed the bean to the infant, poured milk
into the cone, through the bottle like a vase,
and thought of building trees. The key in the door,
the metallic grind and grit and click, the husband's hand stopped
as he hears the crunch in the snow not from boot or paw
but hoof—the deer, his eye a brown lagoon
where the day-sayer sits. His fur, velvet at the spot
above his left hip, haunch, whichever word
suggests animal more than that which, to this man,
is worthy of love—
his fur honeyed through his form until the tangle at the thigh
from the gun.

The baby points east through the trees.
He sees the soft wash and cannot understand what he sees.
His tongue clicks, "Iloc."
If his father turns his heel in the snow
and sees the black skin around the deer's eye, and listens,
he will know what is to become of his son,
who feeds eagerly from glass cups of pumpkin
and green bean, and potato, who cannot bite into anything
with his mouth like a smoothed cave.
These sweet articles: his cupped hand, his lips
in constant prayer, their attempted translation of
his sounds into something true: his coos becoming
"eel" and "grace" (or "grays," because they had
hoped he would be a visual child, would learn
through sight).

So speak, he whispers to the long snout,
freckled with white. The hooves turn, flee,
the carrier bounding into the east.
The husband turns the brass key, forgets
the encounter. The baby stretches his
round arms toward his father and flexes his
thick fingers in eagerness, his shoulders hunched
up, his smile the smile of pure love. There is
no chance for change. Through the trees, May
and its river wait, intent.

Doctor

Jeffrey's friends are dying.

Doze's ribcage is an icehouse where pierced
fish look through bone bars, a jail. A warm wife up
the forest road heats a pie in her gingham apron.
Man and dog hit frost. She and the oven bake
a polar opposite, a charged pastry that pulls
toward the lake. Between them a field, a current,
all electric.

She is the antithesis of his drowning. His drowning
is clean, a crisp icicle. It is neatly pressed into the crust. Jeffrey calls,
lonely Jeffrey, he has just lost Nisan, has found him blue in bed.
The housekeeper is called, the police are called, the children
sleep in racecar beds. Doze's warm wife is lost
in this story, no story brings comfort. Jeffrey with his MD
pulls out his prescription pad. Also: Robert, seizing, blastoma
blooming near his eye, gets two weeks to live. Jeffrey with his MD
gives medicine that births delusions of health. Delusion is a soft baby,
a peach fuzz consciousness. Anxiety is an ice floe melting.
The will of a cell's division. How the body turns against itself,
how the doctor turns it halfway back, like a clock.

Dark Miracle

A portion of the roof collapsed, pinning the firefighter to the attic stairwell, leaving him without air. Though he was eventually rescued, he remained in a vegetative state for nine years. In the ninth year of his coma, a level of consciousness unexpectedly returned. He suddenly asked for his wife.

I.

I call it *dark*
for these cross-sections of blood, useless,
platelets failing, where not even calcium

can reveal this one mystery of brain and nerve

and fluid

I call it *dark*,
for the man who returns from ten years of sleep
is a child, not Lazarus, was never dead, is no husband

for a wife, is never long

for the world he returns to.

II.

You beautiful thing, I love your curve of smile
in the clipping that says you've died.
If I could bring you back a second time,
I would. You fell from bed and bled

until the ice-cream scoop of a scar
filled with blood, then pushed out
the fledgling memories, little phoenixes
without fruition, until you slept this time

for good. I hate myself for the ease
with which I'm flippant. I am not your wife;
non-wives find joy in the center of your story.
Romantics say, *He has returned.* Miserable, caged-in lovers

wish *for this fresh start.* I knew in the absence of your voice
you were not so well. I was shaking in my boots,
shaking the paper, tiger-eyed, odd predator, I was shouting
in a wild storm: *What words did you utter*

when your eyes opened in new birth? I was hungry,
but no one would throw down some meat.
I knew your toddler had become a young man.

Your youngest knew you as a body
in a bed, the body called Father. I don't care
for second-hand tales: I need your voice.
This is a time of knowing all, and tact

has left me starving. Now your son spoon-feeds
the father who fed him sweet potato
the night the roof sank low. National news picks up
on mother's estrangement, says she always had

a "lack of faith"—as if a seventeen-year-old with an infant
and half-dead husband could tell you
that God is the animal howling in the corridor.
Everyone says he's changed,

and his son once found the nurse bawling on the sofa
because he'd asked her to make love to him,
to please make love
to this man without a wife.

Her Grandfather Filling the Bathtub
Before a Hurricane

She watches as he stops the drain, twists the acrylic,
fills the yellow tub. His horse shivers
in his picture frame, watches from the hallway.
The barometers are dropping. And this room

and its parts: glossy black sinks, little soaps,
drawers lined with flowered paper, lipsticks chalking
with age, a fine powder on everything, and a light-switch cover
where a leering man with a moustache opens his coat for them.

Her grandfather dips his hands in the water, tests the temperature,
but no one will be bathing. She knows he cleans the city's teeth,
files incisors, files folders for young boys and their bubblegum alginate.
Watch how they hide from the rain. Watch now at the bathroom mirror

as he distracts her from the sky, asks to see her bite.
After the tub is full, he washes her hair in the sink,
combs it like plowing. The dark circle snaps the lines,
blacks the house. And now the wind is tossing trees,

rounding the uprooted palms, each bloodless trunk
a bow scraping the strings of power lines,
all hot weather their song, and now she sees each domestic act
and its sad foundation. Like his twisting of the knob

and its impulse: threat of groundwater filth. Electric loss,
the cooling of the stoves. No way to burn themselves clean.

Nineteen
for Max

Brother, your violent life is back.

Now you see the first loss of your life
as the warning. Our mother by the creek:

abandonment you understood even then.
How soft you were at nine,

thinking *at least this is it,*
the final sour taste of the world.

Each birthyear ending in nine
has buckshot in its thigh. Last night you were waiting

outside of Zach's house for band practice to start,
pacing by the garage, in the driveway with its highway views.

The doors were locked.
You'd had two good shows in Atlanta

and were chronicling your small and starry fame
when Zach's mother drove up with the keys

and said *Don't go in yet.*
                      Soon the parts of you once left intact

were breaking, and you thought, *again.* They brought him out
and said *troubled, troubled*, and *how strange*

when a singer dies, how the voice just goes like that
and leaves no artifact.

I wanted to write something to comfort you,
but today you asked me what greater comfort is there
than anger and our right to it?

Beginning

In creating, we create an end, equal in force
to the first moments of life, that fervor
which manifests itself before us,

by our hand. Who can know, and not know,
that the joy of falling must precede
the pain of the broken body?

The mother's hand, cooled with sweat, cradles
and dies, the absence of the hand hardened
by its former affection, its ghost red-hot

on the back of the arm. Or the unfolding of arms
in a dark room. The moment bleeding black
until the meeting of mouths ensures that its beauty,

concluding anticipation, will end the heart.

Those first months of creation, we
will be the hill and the bird, one descending into another.

The Brittingham Prize in Poetry

Ronald Wallace, General Editor

Places/Everyone • Jim Daniels
C. K. Williams, Judge, 1985

Talking to Strangers • Patricia Dobler
Maxine Kumin, Judge, 1986

Saving the Young Men of Vienna • David Kirby
Mona Van Duyn, Judge, 1987

Pocket Sundial • Lisa Zeidner
Charles Wright, Judge, 1988

Slow Joy • Stephanie Marlis
Gerald Stern, Judge, 1989

Level Green • Judith Vollmer
Mary Oliver, Judge, 1990

Salt • Renée Ashley
Donald Finkel, Judge, 1991

Sweet Ruin • Tony Hoagland
Donald Justice, Judge, 1992

The Red Virgin: A Poem of Simone Weil • Stephanie Strickland
Lisel Mueller, Judge, 1993

The Unbeliever • Lisa Lewis
Henry Taylor, Judge, 1994

Old and New Testaments • Lynn Powell
Carolyn Kizer, Judge, 1995

Brief Landing on the Earth's Surface • Juanita Brunk
Philip Levine, Judge, 1996

And Her Soul Out of Nothing • Olena Kalytiak Davis
Rita Dove, Judge, 1997

Bardo • Suzanne Paola
Donald Hall, Judge, 1998

A Field Guide to the Heavens • Frank X. Gaspar
Robert Bly, Judge, 1999

A Path between Houses • Greg Rappleye
Alicia Ostriker, Judge, 2000

Horizon Note • Robin Behn
Mark Doty, Judge, 2001

Acts of Contortion • Anna George Meek
Edward Hirsch, Judge, 2002

The Room Where I Was Born • Brian Teare
Kelly Cherry, Judge, 2003

Sea of Faith • John Brehm
Carl Dennis, Judge, 2004

Jagged with Love • Susanna Childress
Billy Collins, Judge, 2005

New Jersey • Betsy Andrews
Linda Gregerson, Judge, 2007

Meditations on Rising and Falling • Philip Pardi
David St. John, Judge, 2008

Bird Skin Coat • Angela Sorby
Marilyn Nelson, Judge, 2009

The Mouths of Grazing Things • Jennifer Boyden
Robert Pinsky, Judge, 2010

Wait • Alison Stine
Cornelius Eady, Judge, 2011

Darkroom • Jazzy Danziger
Jean Valentine, Judge, 2012